Contents

Look what Shabana dug up in her garden.

It was shiny. It felt hard. The edges were sharp.

Shabana put it in her pocket and went into the house.

Inside Dad was washing up.

His hands were slippery. Dad dropped a new saucer. It hit the floor.

Crash! Broken bits went all over the kitchen.

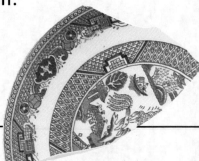

Shabana picked up all the bits she could find.

They were hard. The edges were sharp. The pieces were smooth and shiny.

Shabana tried to fit the bits together.

It was like a jigsaw. One piece said, 'Wedgwood' on the bottom.

Dad said that was the name of the makers.

WEDGWOOD®
Bone China
MADE IN ENGLAND

3

Dad said, "Let's throw it away.
We can buy a new saucer."

Shabana and Dad wrapped the broken bits
in newspaper and put them in the dustbin.

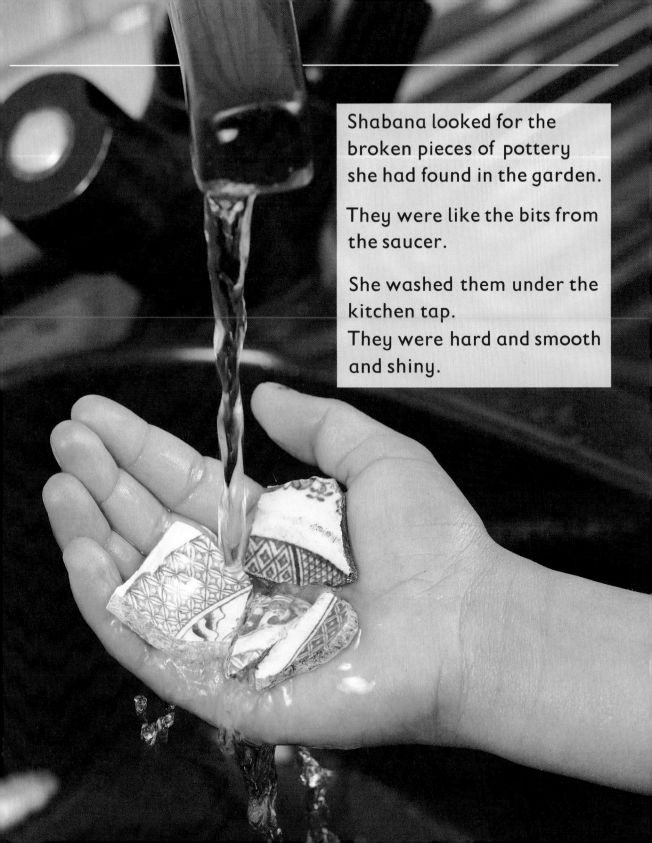

Shabana looked for the broken pieces of pottery she had found in the garden.

They were like the bits from the saucer.

She washed them under the kitchen tap.
They were hard and smooth and shiny.

They looked older than the saucer.

On one piece it said 'Wedgwood', just like the saucer.

On the other side it had a blue pattern.

It was like one of Gran's best plates.

Shabana took her pieces of pottery to school.

Mrs Moorcroft showed them to the class.

How had they got into Shabana's garden?

Christoper's clay tube

On Monday other children brought in things they had found under the ground.

Here they are:

Apshan's glass marble

Sanad's spoon

Sam's coin

Claire's brick

By the end of the week there was a big collection.

The class looked closely at all the things.

Were they shiny or dull?

They felt them.
Were they rough or smooth?
Were they light or heavy?
What were they made from?

They guessed what people used them for.

Where did all these things come from?
How long had they been buried under the ground?

Mrs Moorcroft took Shabana's class to the museum.

The museum had lots of broken pottery.

Some of it was very old.

Each piece had a label.

The curator looked after the museum.
He was called Ian Jones.

Ian said, "I think Shabana's pottery is about one hundred years old.

Let me look for this mark in my book.

Look at this plate. It's like your piece, Shabana."

A Roman bowl

Ian showed them a Roman mixing bowl.
It was thick and rough.

Ian said, "Look at the maker's name.
It's on the rim, not on the bottom.

Once it was used in a kitchen like this."

Roman kitchen, Museum of London

When the Romans broke a bowl two thousand
years ago they threw the pieces in a pit.
They didn't have dustbins.

The pit filled up with earth and rubbish.

The pieces stayed under the ground until
someone found them two thousand years later.

A clay pipe

Ian said all the things Shabana's class had found
had been thrown away or lost by someone in the past.

Christopher's clay tube was a piece of an old pipe.

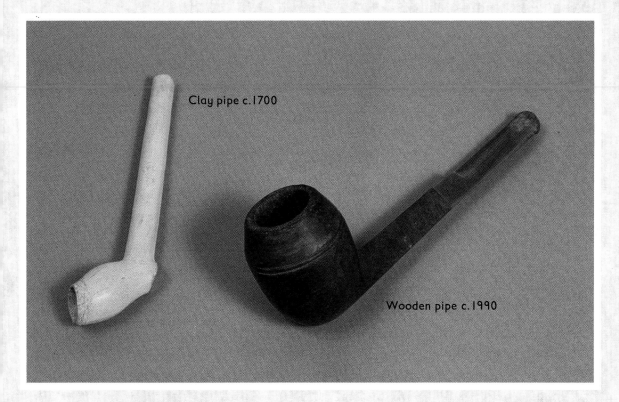

Clay pipe c.1700

Wooden pipe c.1990

Ian showed them a white clay pipe that had been
made three hundred years ago.

Ian said, "Look how small this pipe is.
When this was made people only smoked a little
at a time.
Tobacco was hard to get."

A lemonade bottle

Ian showed them where the round glass marble like Apshan's had come from.

It was in an old glass bottle.

In the past fizzy drinks were only sold in glass bottles not tin cans or plastic bottles.

The bottle was filled with lemonade.

The fizzy gas pushed the marble up to the top of the bottle. This closed the bottle and kept the drink fizzy.

Children broke the bottles to get the marbles out.

How old was Claire's brick?

They saw some old bricks which were thin and crooked.

They had been made by hand. Straw had been put in the clay to help it stick together.

They could see the marks of the straw.

Claire's brick was thicker and more even. There were no straw marks.

The brick was new like her house.

The brick was probably thrown away when Claire's house was being built.

Was Sanad's spoon silver?

Ian looked at the handle.

It said 'EPNS'.

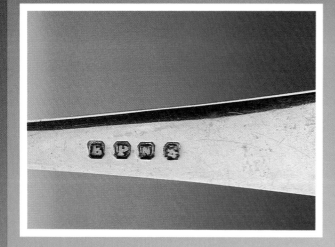

These letters stand for 'Electro Plated Nickel Silver', not real silver.

Ian said, "Let's look at some real silver.

Real silver has a tiny little lion mark on it."

Sam's coin was an old penny.

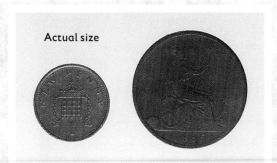

Actual size

Modern and Victorian penny

On one side it said 1885.

Modern and Victorian penny

On the other was the head of Queen Victoria.

She was queen from 1837 to 1901.

Roman waterfront site, Billingsgate, London

Ian said, "Do you know about people whose job it is to dig up old things from under the ground?

They are called archaeologists.

Archaeological excavation at Pudding Lane, London, 1981

The places where archaeologists dig are called excavations."

Ian said, "I want to show you something special.

This was in a house built almost two thousand years ago.

It is called a mosaic floor.

It is made of little coloured stones.

People didn't have carpets then.
In some big houses they had mosaics."

This floor was found by a farmer in a field.

He saw some bits of stone sticking out.

The Bucklersbury Roman Pavement, Museum of London

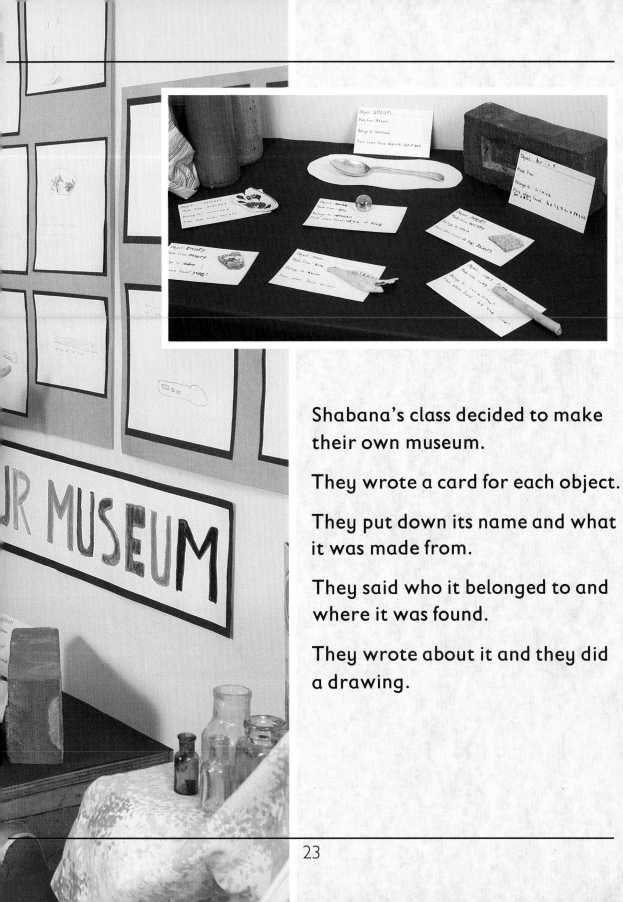

Shabana's class decided to make their own museum.

They wrote a card for each object.

They put down its name and what it was made from.

They said who it belonged to and where it was found.

They wrote about it and they did a drawing.

One night after school they held an exhibition.

There was a big notice saying, 'Our Museum'.

They invited Ian Jones and their parents.

Shabana's Dad came and he was surprised
how much they'd learnt from things that were
found under the ground.